New Getting Into English

Joseph Cronin　Eric Bray

NAN'UN-DO

To the Student

Welcome to *New Getting Into English*. We are confident that you will find this book both very useful and a lot of fun. You will learn useful words, phrases and expressions helping you to express yourself in everyday English communication. The many speaking activities will give you chances to talk about yourself—your family, friends, school, likes and dislikes, and so on—and to steadily build up your English skills.

There are useful pronunciation points in each unit. The good news is that, with a little effort, Japanese-speakers can acquire very satisfactory English pronunciation. There are also listening exercises giving examples of how to do the speaking activities. An important element in learning anything is doing simple things well. Make sure you review things until you are quite fluent.

Download Audio

音声ファイル
無料 DL
のご案内

このテキストの音声を無料で視聴（ストリーミング）・ダウンロードできます。自習用音声としてご活用ください。
以下のサイトにアクセスしてテキスト番号で検索してください。

https://nanun-do.com　テキスト番号［**512077**］

※ 無線 LAN（WiFi）に接続してのご利用を推奨いたします。

※ 音声ダウンロードは Zip ファイルでの提供になります。
お使いの機器によっては別途ソフトウェア（アプリケーション）の導入が必要となります。

Read by
Hannah Grace
Josh Keller

※ New Getting Into English 音声ダウンロードページは
以下の QR コードからもご利用になれます。

Table of Contents

Unit 1

Hi, I'm Rina.

1 **Practice this conversation with a partner. Then practice it again using your own name.**

A: Hi, I'm Rina.

B: Hi, Rina. I'm Shota.

A: Nice to meet you.

B: Nice to meet *you*.

2 Pronunciation: **Some Japanese names are difficult for English speakers. How might English speakers pronounce these?**

Marina	Tomoko	Mayumi
Kyoka	Tokyo	Kyoto
Ryo	Ryu	

3 Speaking: **Here are some common English first names. Which are girl's names? Which are boy's names? Write the word girl or boy in the blanks.**

A: Jacob is a boy's name.

B: I think Emma is a girl's name.

Jacob	______	Emma	______	Michael	______
Joshua	______	Daniel	______	Olivia	______
Hannah	______	Emily	______	Matthew	______
Andrew	______	Sophia	______	Ashley	______

4 Speaking: **Practice this conversation with a partner. Then practice it again using a different English name.**

A: Hi, I'm Joshua.

B: Hi, Joshua. I'm Ashley.

A: Ashley. Nice to meet you.

English names often have short forms.

Susan—Sue—Suzy Jennifer—Jen—Jenny

James—Jim—Jimmy Nicholas—Nick—Nicky

5 Vocabulary: **Here are the names of some common university majors (*senko*) in English. Write the Japanese words for the majors on the lines. Write your major, too.**

economics	________	law	________	sociology	________
psychology	________	music	________	engineering	________
medicine	________	German	________	*your major*	________

A: What does economics mean?

B: Uh, *keizaigaku*.

A: How do you say *keizaigaku* in English?

B: Uh, economics.

6 Speaking: **Practice the conversation. Then make up new conversations using your own information.**

A: Hi, my name's Genta.

B: Genta. I'm Saya.

A: Saya. What do you do?

B: I'm a student. My major is Economics. How about you?

A: My major is English. I'm a first-year student.

7 **Pronunciation:** **Be careful not to add an 'o' sound to words such as 'and,' 'but' or 'right,' or a 'u' sound to words such as 'like' or 'big.' First practice slow pronunciation of these expressions. Then practice faster pronunciation.**

8

Tea and toast.	Fish and chips.	Nice but expensive.
It's on the right.	I like fish.	She's about 25.

8 **Speaking:** **Practice the conversation. Then practice it again using your own information.**

9

A: Do you have any brothers or sisters?

B: Yes. I have an older brother. He's 23.

A: I see. And what does he do?

B: Well, he works for a small company in Nagoya.
It's a delivery company.

A: I see.

B: How about you? Any brothers or sisters?

A: No. I'm an only child.

9 **Listening:** **Listen to Kotaro and Mutsumi getting to know each other. Fill in the information.**

10

a. What do Kotaro's parents do?

____

b. Does Mutsumi's mother work?

____

c. Does Mutsumi have any brothers or sisters?

____

d. What does Kotaro's brother do?

____

e. Is Mutsumi in a club or circle?

____

10 Speaking: **Find out about your partner's family. Write notes using your partner's answers to these questions.**

a. What do your parents do?

____

b. Does your mother work?

____

c. Do you have any brothers or sisters?

____

d. What does he/she do? What do they do?

____

e. Are you in a club or circle?

____

Useful Language

He works for a company.
She has her own business.
He has his own business.
She's a housewife/a homemaker.

11 Speaking: **Now meet with another pair and introduce your partner using the notes in Activity 10.**

Unit 2 How do you spell that?

1 Pronunciation: **The name of the letter C is pronounced /si:/ not like Japanese *shi* /ʃi/. The word "sister" is pronounced /sɪstər/ not like *shisuta* /ʃisuta:/.**

11

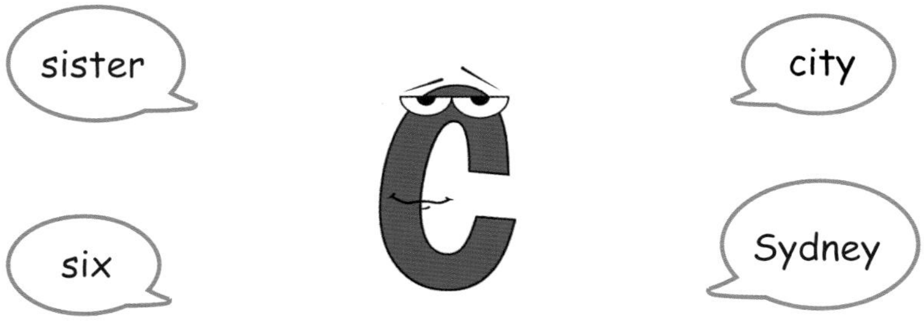

2 **Practice the conversation with a partner.**

12

A: Can I get your telephone number?
B: Just a minute. It's 090-825-3665.
A: Uh-huh. 090-825...
B: 3665.
A: Got it.

> **Pronunciation Point**
> O is pronounced /oʊ/
> or zero /zi:roʊ/

3 Pronunciation: **The pronunciation of the letter 't' is often influenced by surrounding sounds.**

13

What part? /whappart/ What color? /whakkolor/
eight two /eittu:/ eight eight /eɪteɪt/
first name last name postcard

4 Listening: **Write the numbers you hear on the lines below.**

14

a. ______ b. ______ c. ______ d. ______
e. ______ f. ______ g. ______ h. ______
i. ______ j. ______ k. ______ l. ______
m. __________ n. __________ o. __________
p. ________________ q. ________________

> **Useful Classroom Language**
> Your turn. / My turn.
> Okay? / Okay.
> I'll be A, you be B.

5 **Work with a partner. Student A dictates to Student B and Student B writes the numbers he/she hears.**

Student A

_____ _____ _____ _____ _____	76, 35, 08, 92, 41
_____ _____ _____ _____	981, 704, 632, 715
_______ _______ _______	7214, 3890, 6631
___________ ___________	090-7931-8462, 302-7864

Student B

_____ _____ _____ _____ _____	79, 82, 38, 50, 63
_____ _____ _____ _____	923, 104, 551, 896
_______ _______ _______	7895, 3264, 8812
___________ ___________	080-931-7662, 7754-8321

6 **With a partner decide who is Student A and who is Student B. Then practice the model conversation. Ask and answer in turns for the missing numbers in your list below. Write the numbers on the lines.**

15

A: Can you give me Joe's number? (or) Do you know Joe's number?
B: Joe's number? Yes. It's ... 764-8321.
A: 764 ...
B: 8321.
A: OK. Got it. (or) OK. Thanks.

Student A		Student B	
Joe	764-8321	Joe	764-8321
Mark	___________	Mark	070-901-5632
Kazuo	897-7621	Kazuo	___________
Yukie	___________	Yukie	075-751-6624
Joshua	080-585-3088	Joshua	___________
Nancy	___________	Nancy	090-278-6352
Emma	872-6521	Emma	___________
Kevin	___________	Kevin	692-7854
Sophia	03-9498-5014	Sophia	___________

7 Listening: **Practice saying the following letters: C, F, V, W, Z. Listen and write the words your teacher spells.**

16

1. ________________ 2. ________________ 3. ________________

4. ________________ 5. ________________ 6. ________________

7. ________________ 8. ________________ 9. ________________

10. ________________ 11. ________________ 12. ________________

8 Speaking: **Student B should close his/her book. Student A should ask how to spell the words in Activity 7. Then change roles.**

17

A: How do you spell 'snake'?

B: Snake? Uh, S-N-A-K-E?

A: Yeah, that's right./Wrong.

9 Speaking: **Practice the conversation.**

18

A: Can you spell your first name?

B: H-A-R-U-K-A.

A: And your last name?

B: K-A-M-I-M-U-R-A.

A: What's your phone number?

B: 090-872-9910.

A: OK. Thanks.

10 Listening: Listen and write what you hear in the blanks.

19

	First Name	Last Name	Phone number
1.			
2.			

11 Speaking: Find out about other students, using the conversation in Activity 9 as a model.

Make up a phone number: ______________________ （架空の電話番号を記載してください）

	First Name	Last Name	Phone number
1.			
2.			
3.			
4.			
5.			
6.			
7.			
8.			

Unit 3 What's the time?

1

Pronunciation: The pronunciation of numbers is a little difficult.
Put the stress on the correct part of the word.

20

13	thirTEEN	30	THIRty	14	fourTEEN	40	FORty
15	fifTEEN	50	FIFty	16	sixTEEN	60	SIXty

15 minutes FIFteen minutes   50 minutes FIFty minutes

16 people SIXteen people   60 people SIXty people

2

Practice these ways of asking the time.

21

Polite: used with strangers

- Excuse me. Do you have the time?
- Could you tell me the time please?

Informal: used with people you know

- What time is it?
- What's the time?

3

Match the times to the clocks. Then practice saying the times.

22

a. 8:00 eight (o'clock)

b. 9:10 nine ten

c. 11:15 eleven fifteen

d. 12:30 twelve thirty

e. 1:40 one forty

f. 2:45 two forty-five

g. 3:05 three oh five

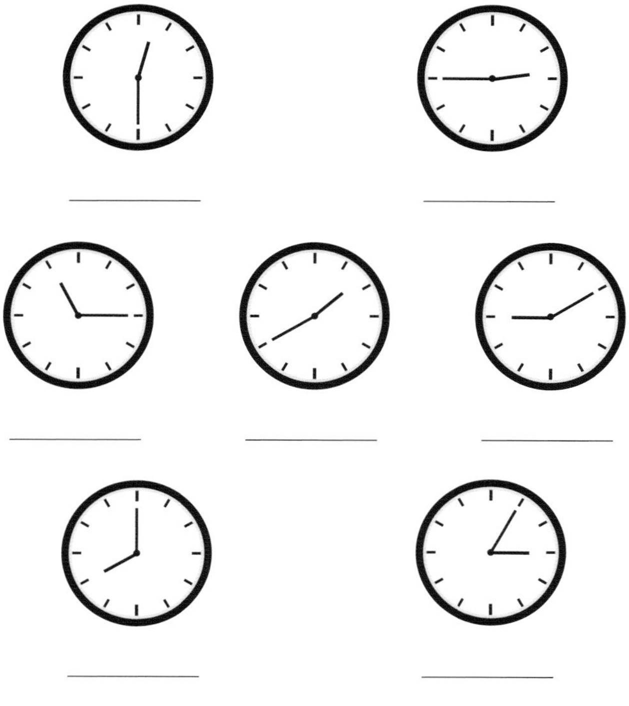

4 Pronunciation: Practice pronouncing the *schwa* sound /ə/ in the underlined syllables.

23

nine o'clock   twelve o'clock   a cup of coffee   He's at work.

5 Listening: Listen and write the times you hear on the lines below.

24

1. ________	2. ________	3. ________
4. ________	5. ________	6. ________
7. ________	8. ________	9. ________
10. ________	11. ________	12. ________

6 Speaking: Choose who is A and B. Dictate the times to your partner.

Student A

1. 5:10	2. 3:30	3. 4:15	4. 8:05	5. 1:55
6. 7:40	7. 6:25	8. 9:15	9. 9:50	10. the time now
1. ______	2. ______	3. ______	4. ______	5. ______
6. ______	7. ______	8. ______	9. ______	10. ______

Student B

1. 7:20	2. 2:45	3. 6:15	4. 9:30	5. 1:25
6. 5:00	7. 6:50	8. 4:30	9. 8:35	10. the time now
1. ______	2. ______	3. ______	4. ______	5. ______
6. ______	7. ______	8. ______	9. ______	10. ______

7 Practice the conversation. Then use the times in Activity 3 to make more conversations.

25

A: When's the next express train?

B: It's in 20 minutes, at 5:30.

A: Thanks. I'd better run.
See you tomorrow.

B: See you.

8 **Write the names of the missing days of the week in the spaces.**

Days of the Week

____

Tuesday

____

____

____

Saturday

____

9 **Can you make true sentences for yourself? Practice saying them to a partner.**
Example: I get up early on Monday.

a. I get up early on ____________________

b. I have three classes on ____________________

c. I only have one class in the afternoon on ____________________

d. I go to my club/part-time job on ____________________

e. I watch TV in the evening on ____________________

f. My favorite day of the week is ____________________

10 Listening: **Listen to Michael and Emily's conversation. Write answers to the questions in the spaces.**

26

a. What's Emily's busiest day? ____________________

b. How many classes does Michael have on Tuesday? ____________________

c. What time does Emily get up? ____________________

d. How does Emily come to school? ____________________

e. What time does Michael get home? ____________________

11 Speaking: **First, think about your busiest school day. Then, answer the questions by writing your own information. Then interview partners and write their answers in the spaces below.**

a. What's your busiest day? ______________________________

b. What time do you get up? ______________________________

c. How do you come to school? ______________________________

d. Where do you have lunch? ______________________________

e. What time do you get home? ______________________________

f. What's your favorite day of the week? ______________________________

	Partner's name	busiest day	gets up at	comes to school by	has lunch	gets home at	favorite day
1.							
2.							
3.							
4.							
5.							
6.							

Unit 4

Where are you from?

1 Pronunciation: **Practice pronouncing these words containing the schwa /ə/ sound.**

27

Jəpan	Kərea	Pəru	Cənadiən
Japənese	Itəly	Canəda	

2 **Draw lines to match these cities and countries. Then practice the conversation below with a partner using different cities and countries.**

28

Cities	Countries
Cairo	Korea
Paris	Italy
Rome	Egypt
Los Angeles	Canada
Seoul	China
Vancouver	Thailand
Dublin	the USA
Bangkok	France
Sydney	Ireland
Madrid	Australia
Beijing	Spain

A: Where's Paris?

B: Paris? It's in France. OK, where's Vancouver?

A: I think it's in Canada.

3 Speaking: **Practice this conversation with a partner.**

29

A: Where are you from?

B: I'm from France.

A: Oh, really? *Where* in France?

B: I'm from Paris. Where are *you* from?

A: I'm from Vancouver, Canada.

B: Vancouver. I see.

4

Draw lines to match the towns and prefectures. Then practice the conversation below with a partner using different towns and prefectures.

30

Towns	Prefectures
Hirosaki	Hyogo
Takatsuki	Okinawa
Matsuyama	Shizuoka
Beppu	Aomori
Kobe	Ehime
Hakodate	Oita
Hamamatsu	Hokkaido
Kamakura	Osaka
Naha	Kanagawa

A: Where's Hirosaki?

B: Hirosaki? Um, it's in Aomori.
Where's Naha?

A: It's in Okinawa prefecture.

5

Speaking: **Practice this conversation with a partner. Then practice it again using your own hometown and prefecture.**

31

A: Where are you from?

B: I'm from Aomori Prefecture.

A: *Where* in Aomori?

B: Hirosaki.

A: I see.

B: How about *you*? Where are *you* from?

A: I'm from Kamakura in Kanagawa Prefecture.

Hirosaki

Kamakura

<u>Common Error</u>

Remember: A prefecture is not a hometown.

Wrong: My hometown is Aichi.

Correct: My hometown is Kariya in Aichi Prefecture.

6 Speaking: Look at the map. Then practice this conversation with a partner. Next, make up new conversations using different cities.

32

A: Where's Wakayama?

B: It's south of Osaka.

Where's Kyoto?

A: It's west of Nagoya.

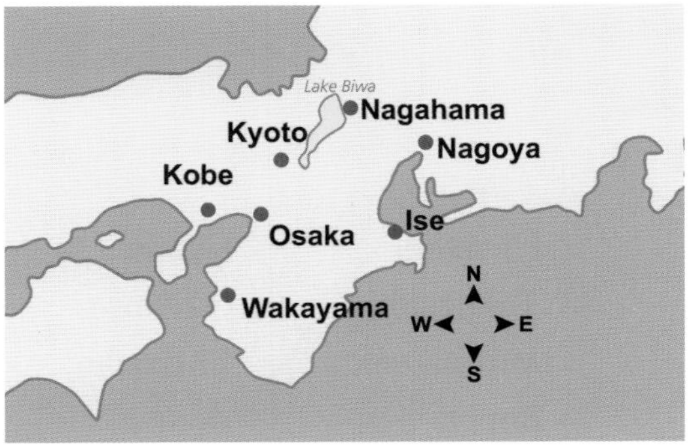

7 Match these descriptions with the cities in the box below. Write the names of the cities on the lines.

a. This city is south of Kyoto, about an hour on the train. __________
b. This city is in the western part of Honshu, near Kyushu. __________
c. This city is east of Kanazawa, about an hour by car. __________
d. This city is about 90 minutes by bullet train north of Tokyo. __________
e. This city is in the western part of Hokkaido. __________

Sendai	Toyama	Nara	Yamaguchi	Sapporo

Write similar sentences about two places you know. Write their names on the lines. Then read the sentences to your group members and have them guess your cities.

1. ____________________
__________ City __________
2. ____________________
__________ City __________

8 Pronunciation: How would an English speaker with no Japanese pronounce these Japanese place names?

33

Narita	Nagoya	Osaka	Hiroshima
Kyoto	Tokyo	Kobe	

9 Kyoto is famous for its many temples. What places can you think of for these?

a. __________ is famous for its castle.
b. __________ is famous for its giant statue of the Buddha.
c. __________ is known for its white peaches.
d. __________ is known for Lake Biwa.
e. __________ is well-known for its beef.

What's your town or city famous for? ____________________

10 Listening: **Aki talks to Junya about her hometown. Write answers to the questions in the spaces.**

34

a. Where in Nara does Aki live? ______________________

b. What's the population of Nara city? ______________________

c. What does she like about Nara? ______________________

d. Where was her high school trip to? ______________________

e. What did she enjoy doing on her trip? ______________________

11 Speaking: **In pairs, talk about your hometowns. Write what your partner says in the spaces.**

a. Where were you born? ______________________

b. Where did you grow up? ______________________

c. Can you draw a map to show me where you're from? ______________________

d. What do you like about your hometown? ______________________

e. What's it famous for? ______________________

Is there a famous temple or shrine? ______________________

Are there any other sightseeing attractions? ______________________

Is there a festival? ______________________

f. What's the population? ______________________

g. Is there a famous food? ______________________

h. Where else have you been in Japan? ______________________

i. Would you like to live somewhere else? ______________________

Useful Language

The population of Saga Prefecture is about 850,000.

The population of Saga City is about 230,000.

Write in the population of your city and prefecture. Can you say this number in English?

City name	____________	Population	____________
Prefecture name	____________	Population	____________

Unit 5 What's your favorite food?

1 Vocabulary: **Do you know these foods? Circle the words you know. Then write two more words for each food group.**

Food Groups

Vegetables	Fruits	Fish	Meat	Grains
spinach	strawberries	tuna	beef	rice
lettuce	apples	salmon	pork	bread
leek	tangerines	squid	chicken	pasta
radish	grapes	mackerel	lamb	noodles
________	________	________	________	________
________	________	________	________	________

2 **With a partner, make up and practice conversations like this one using all the foods in Activity 1. One person should ask questions and the other person should close the book and try to answer.**

35

A: What's spinach in Japanese?
B: Spinach is *horenso* in Japanese.
A: Oh, I see.
What are grapes in Japanese?
B: Grapes are *budo*.

3 **Draw lines to match the foods with the name of the dish they are used in.**

Foods (Ingredients)	Name of the Dish
1. potato, onion, beef, salt	pizza
2. flour, sausage, cheese, tomato sauce	spaghetti carbonara
3. cabbage, flour, egg, pork	*niku jaga*
4. pasta, bacon, milk, black pepper	*okonomiyaki*

4 Listening: **Your teacher will name some ingredients that are used to make a popular dish. Listen and write them on the lines below. Then guess the name of the dish.**

36

Ingredients

- ☐ ____________________
- ☐ ____________________
- ☐ ____________________
- ☐ ____________________
- ☐ ____________________

Name of the dish: ______________

5 **Think of a dish you like. Write the ingredients used to make the dish on the lines below. Then, in a small group, tell the other members what your ingredients are and ask them to guess the dish they are used in. Use the conversation below as a model.**

37

Ingredients: __________, __________, __________, __________, __________

A: The ingredients in this dish are __________, __________, __________, __________, and __________.
Can you guess what dish it is?

B: Is it ______________?

A: No, it isn't. Try again.

C: Is it ______________?

A: You got it!

6 Pronunciation: **Pronouns are usually not stressed. Practice saying these sentences.**

38

Do you **make** it?

She **likes** it.

He **drinks** it.

What does she **eat**?

Does he speak **English**?

7 Vocabulary: Look at the list of drinks in the box and add some drinks of your own. Which ones do you sometimes drink?

DRINKS

• coffee	• black tea	• barley tea	• juice
• soft drink	• bubble tea	• milk	• mineral water
• ________	• ________	• ________	• ________

8 Listening: What do they like to eat and drink? Write down the answers to these questions.

39

a. What does Emily drink at breakfast? ______________________

b. What does Matthew drink at breakfast? ______________________

c. What does Emily drink in the afternoon? ______________________

d. What kind of vegetables does Emily like? ______________________

e. What kind of vegetables does Matthew like? ______________________

f. What kind of fruit does Emily like? ______________________

g. Is there any food Matthew doesn't like? ______________________

Useful Language

I like	the taste.
I don't like	the smell.
	the texture.

9 Speaking: **Interview three partners and write their answers to the questions in the spaces.**

Questions	Partner 1 (Name:______)	Partner 2 (Name:______)	Partner 3 (Name:______)
a. What do you drink at breakfast?	__________	__________	__________
b. What do you drink during the day?	__________	__________	__________
c. What drinks do you not like?	__________	__________	__________
d. What vegetables do you like?	__________	__________	__________
e. What kinds of fruit/meat do you like?	__________	__________	__________
f. What kind of sushi do you like best?	__________	__________	__________
g. Are there any foods you don't like?	__________	__________	__________

Unit 6

How often do you get your hair cut?

1 Vocabulary: Write the names of the missing months in the spaces.

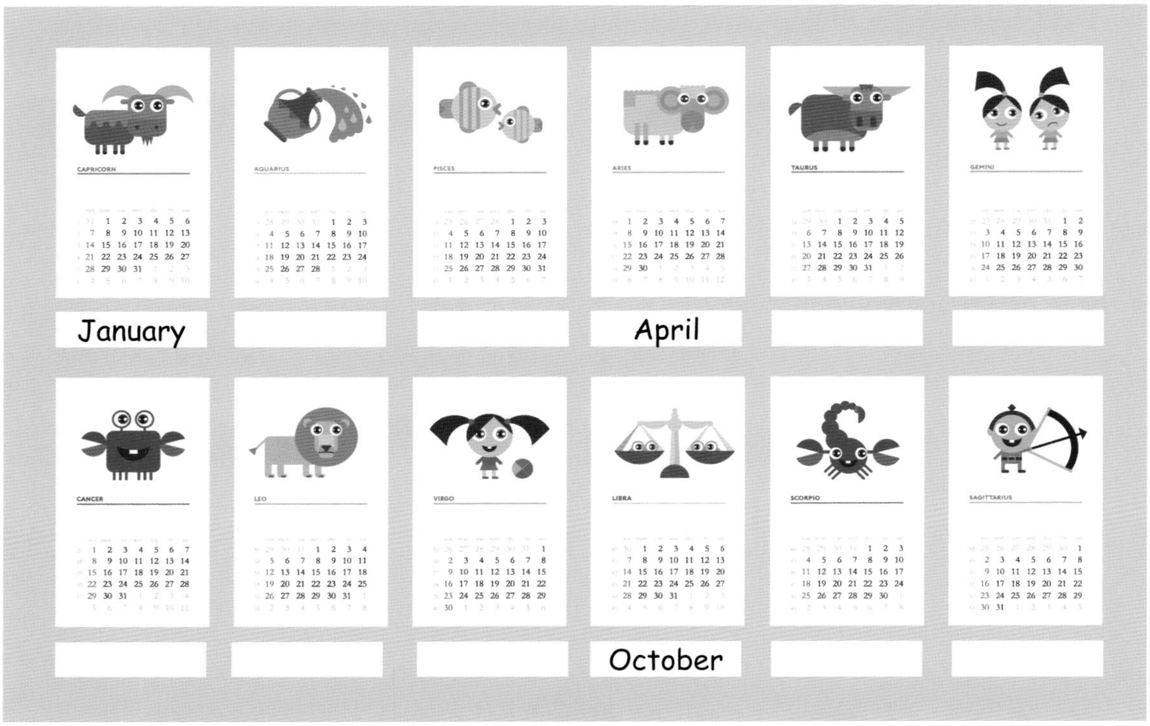

Useful Language

I was born in 2004.
Eri's birthday is in April.
I was born on May 10th.

2 Practice saying these dates.

January 3, 1995	*say*	January third, nineteen ninety-five
October 22, 2004	*say*	October twenty-second, two thousand and four
6/5/2010	*say*	June fifth, twenty ten
8/24/2025	*say*	August twenty-fourth, twenty twenty-five

3 Listening: Listen and write the dates you hear.

40

1. ______ 2. ______ 3. ______ 4. ______
5. ______ 6. ______ 7. ______ 8. ______
9. ______ 10. ______

4 Decide which person is Student A and B. Dictate these dates to your partner and write the dates you hear in the blanks. If you are A, cover B, if you are B, cover A.

Student A

1. August 9th 2. February 3rd 3. July 25th 4. September 16th
5. March 8th 6. November 1st 7. May 2nd 8. December 31st
9. Eiichi Shibusawa was born in 1840 and died in 1931.

1. ______ 2. ______ 3. ______
4. ______ 5. ______ 6. ______
7. ______ 8. ______
9. Umeko Tsuda born: ______ died: ______

Student B

1. ______ 2. ______ 3. ______
4. ______ 5. ______ 6. ______
7. ______ 8. ______
9. Eiichi Shibusawa born: ______ died: ______

1. May 10th 2. August 13th 3. May 1st 4. January 22nd
5. August 28th 6. June 10th 7. July 5th 8. September 3rd
9. Umeko Tsuda was born in 1864 and died in 1929.

5 Listening: Write what Riku and Eri say in the spaces.

41

a. Today's date is ______
b. Riku's birthday is ______
c. Eri's birthday is ______
d. Eri's cousin's birthday is on ______
e. Riku's favorite month is ______
f. Eri's least favorite month is ______
g. Riku and Eri were born in the year ______

6 Speaking: Talk to three students and write their answers in the spaces.

Questions	Student 1	Student 2	Student 3
a. What's today's date?			
b. When's your birthday?			
c. Do you know anybody who has a birthday this month?			
d. When's your mother's/father's/sister's/brother's birthday?			
e. What's your favorite month?			
f. What year were you born?			
g. What year will you graduate?			

7 Grammar: Frequency adverbs are used to tell how often we do certain things. For example, the adverb "always" means "100% of the time." Draw lines between the adverbs on the left with their frequencies in % on the right.

Adverb	Frequency in %
always	1-5%
never	5-15%
usually	0%
often	60-90%
sometimes	100%
once in a while	20-50%
hardly ever	80-90%

8 Write a frequency adverb on each line to make the sentence true for you.

a. I ______________ get up before 7 a.m.

b. I ______________ cook.

c. I ______________ ride a bicycle.

d. I ______________ go to see a movie.

e. I ______________ sleep in past 11 a.m. on Sunday morning.

f. I ______________ go to bed after 1 a.m.

Common Error

"Sometimes" means *tokidoki*: We sometimes meet for lunch.

"Sometime" means *itsuka*: Let's meet for lunch sometime.

9 Speaking: **Practice this conversation with a partner. Then use the sentences you completed in Activity 8 to make more conversations.**

42

A: How often do you get up before 7 a.m.?

B: I sometimes get up before 7 a.m.
How about you?

A: I never get up before 7 a.m.

B: Oh, I see.

10 Listening: **Listen to Daniel and Emma's conversation. Write answers to the questions in the spaces.**

43

a. How often does Daniel go to see a movie? ______

b. How often does Emma go to see a movie? ______

c. How often does Emma ride a bicycle? ______

d. How often does Daniel ride a bicycle? ______

e. How often does Emma watch TV? ______

11 Speaking: **First, use the frequency adverbs in Activity 7 to show how often you do the activities. Write your answers in the spaces. Then, in a small group, find out how often the other members do the activities and write their answers in the spaces.**

How often do you ...?	You	Partner 1 (Name:______)	Partner 2 (Name:______)	Partner 3 (Name:______)
... go to see a movie?	______	______	______	______
... ride a bicycle?	______	______	______	______
... get your hair cut?	______	______	______	______
... watch TV?	______	______	______	______
... catch a cold?	______	______	______	______
... go to karaoke?	______	______	______	______

Unit 7 What kinds of music do you like?

1 Pronunciation: **Listen for the difference in pronunciation between can and can't in the pairs of sentences below. Practice saying the sentences after you hear them.**

44

can /kən/	can't /kǽnt/
I can do it.	I can't do it.
I can swim.	I can't swim.
She can win.	She can't win.
He can help you.	He can't help you.

Which sentence do you hear? Check the box.

1. ☐ I can imagine. ☐ I can't imagine.
2. ☐ I can drive. ☐ I can't drive.
3. ☐ You can do it. ☐ You can't do it.
4. ☐ He can play golf. ☐ He can't play golf.

2 Vocabulary: **Draw lines to match the music genre on the left with the musicians/groups on the right. Then compare your answers with a partner.**

45

A: Rock is the Beatles and Led Zeppelin.
B: J-Pop is ...

Genre	Musicians/Group
Rock	Justin Bieber, Billie Eilish
J-Pop	Drake, Jay-Z
Western pop	Kiyoshi Hikawa, Aki Yashiro
Classical	AKB48, Perfume
Rap/Hip hop	Blackpink, Girls' Generation
Enka	The Beatles, Led Zeppelin
K-Pop	Mozart, Chopin

3 Speaking: **Listen and practice with a partner.**

46

A: What's your favorite kind of music?

B: Uh, I like J-Pop and K-Pop.

A: Me too. So, who's your favorite musician or artist?

B: I like Blackpink. Their dancing is great. Who do you like?

A: I also like Western pop. I like Lady Gaga. I often sing her songs at karaoke.

4 Speaking: **First, practice the patterns in the box for talking about musicians you like or dislike. Next, practice this conversation with a partner. Then write the names of two musicians/groups you like and two you don't like on the lines below. Practice the conversation again using those names.**

47

A: What do you think of Exile?

B: Hmm, I don't really like them.

A: I don't, either.

B: How do you like sumika?

A: They're pretty good.
I really like their new song.

B: Yeah. I do, too.

Like/Dislike Patterns

+++ They're great!
+++ I love their music!
++ I really like them/him/her.
\+ They're pretty good.

0 I've never heard them/him/her.
0 They're OK.

\- They're not so good.
-- I don't really like them/him/her.
--- I can't stand them/him/her.
--- I hate them/him/her.

Like	Dislike
________________	________________
________________	________________

5 Vocabulary: **Match the musical instruments in the box with the pictures below.**

Musical Instruments

harmonica	flute	saxophone	trombone
electric guitar	violin	acoustic guitar	
drums	bass	piano	

Pronunciation: acoustic /əkúːstɪk/

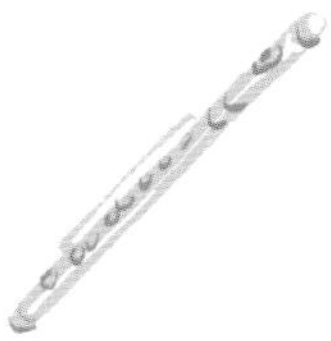

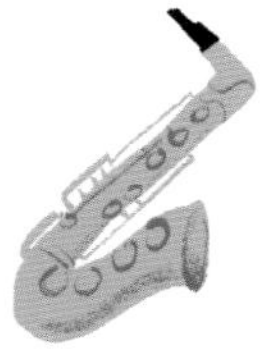

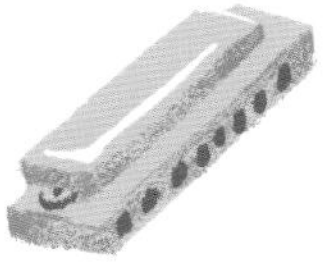

6 Pronunciation: **Before a vowel, most native English-speakers pronounce 'the' as /ði/. Listen and practice.**

48

the afternoon	the evening	the end
the earth	the electric guitar	the ingredients

7 Speaking: **Practice the conversation. Then practice it again using your own information.**

49

A: Are you musical? Can you play an instrument?

B: In my family we're all pretty musical. We all play an instrument.
I play guitar, acoustic guitar. How about you?

A: My mother plays the piano but I can't play an instrument.
When I go to karaoke I always feel I can't sing well.

B: I see.

8 Listening: **Daniel and Ashley talk about music. Listen to their conversation and write the answers to these questions in the blanks.**

50

a. What kinds of music does Daniel like? ______________________________

b. What kinds of music does Ashley like? ______________________________

c. Can Ashley play an instrument? ______________________________

d. Can Daniel play an instrument? ______________________________

9 Speaking: **In groups of four, ask each other these questions. Write your partners' answers in the spaces. Then report to a new partner.**

Questions	You	Partner 1 (Name:______)	Partner 2 (Name:______)	Partner 3 (Name:______)
a. Can you play a musical instrument?				
b. How long have you been playing it?				
c. How about your family or friends?				
d. Does anyone you know play in a band?				
e. Do you have any CD's?				
f. What's your favorite music genre?				
g. What band or musician do you like a lot?				
h. What kind of music do you dislike?				

Unit 8 Who's older, you or your sister?

1 Pronunciation: **English 'h' is a light sound. It often disappears in 'he,' 'him' and 'her.' Listen and practice these expressions.**

51

how   whole   Who is it?   hood

Does (h)e work?   Tell (h)im to go.   Tell (h)er to try.

2 Speaking: **First practice the conversation below. Then, make up conversations about your family using this model.**

52

Wrong	Correct
I have four families.	There are four people in my family.
	There are four of us in my family.

A: There are four people in my family: my mother, my father, my sister and me.

B: Who's older, you or your sister?

A: I'm two years older. How about in *your* family?

B: There are just three of us. My mother, my father and me.
I'm an only child.

A: I see. What's your mother's name?

B: It's Akane.

3 Grammar: **Fill in the missing forms of the adjectives.**

big	bigger	biggest
cute	________	________
tall	________	________
shy	________	________
quiet	________	________
popular	________	________
talkative	________	________
good	________	________

4 Grammar: **Practice saying sentences using these patterns.**

I'm	a little	older / taller / smarter.
She's	a bit	better at English.
He's	a lot	more talkative.
	much	

5 Speaking: **Practice the conversation. Then make up new ones using this pattern. Ask these questions: Who's older/taller/smarter/better at English/more talkative?**

53

A: I'll tell you about my friend Kazue.

B: Kazue. Who's older?

A: Uh, she's a little older – about two months.

B: Two months? Hmm.
Who's more talkative?

A: More talkative? Well, we're about the same.

B: You're both talkative. I see. So who's taller?

A: She's a little taller – about two centimeters.

B: And who's smarter?

A: Me, of course.

6 Pronunciation: **When pronouns are very important, we stress them for emphasis. Listen and practice.**

54

I'll start.

You start.

My turn.

Your turn.

What did *he* say?

How did *you* feel?

7 Speaking: **Practice the conversation.**

55

A: Which is colder, January or February?

B: Uh, that's a difficult one.
I think January is a little colder.

A: Really? I think February is a little colder.

B: Uh, which do you like better, tea or coffee?

A: I prefer tea. Coffee is too bitter for me.

B: Really? I like coffee better. I drink it at breakfast every day.

Common Mistake

× Which do you like, tea or coffee?

✓ Which do you like better, tea or coffee?

8 Listening: **Hayato and Hinata talk about a few topics. Write the answers to the questions in the blanks.**

56

a. Who's taller, Hayato or his father? ______________________________

b. Who's taller, Hinata or her mother? ______________________________

c. Who's the best at English in Hayato's family? ______________________________

d. Which does Hayato like better, rice or bread? ______________________________

e. Which does Hinata prefer, rice or bread? ______________________________

9 Speaking: **Decide who is Student A and Student B. Cover your partner's section and take turns asking and answering the questions.**

Student A

a. Which is colder, January or February?

____

b. Who's better at English, you or your mother?

____

c. Who's the tallest in your family?

____

d. Which do you like better, spring or fall?

____

e. Is Kyushu bigger than Shikoku?

____

f. Which do you prefer, a Japanese or a Western-style breakfast?

____

g. What's the most popular sport in the world?

____

Student B

a. Which is the hottest month in Japan?

____

b. Is your father older than your mother?

____

c. Which do you like better, playing sports or watching them?

____

d. Which do you prefer, tea or coffee?

____

e. Who's the most famous Japanese person in the world?

____

f. Who's better at English, you or me?

____

g. Which do you like better, Tokyo or Osaka?

____

Unit 9 How was your weekend?

1 Grammar: **We form the past tense of English verbs differently, depending on the type of verb. With regular verbs, we just add "ed" to the verb base form. Irregular verbs, however, have many different past tense forms. Write the past tense forms of these regular and irregular verbs in the spaces. Add two more of each type of verb.**

Regular Verbs		Irregular Verbs	
Base form	Past tense	Base form	Past tense
talk	talked	go	went
listen	listened	eat	ate
cook		buy	
want		take	
clean		make	
walk		get	
watch		is	
play		have	
ask		sleep	
work		see	

2 Pronunciation: **Practice pronouncing sentences using past tense forms. Notice what happens when we speak very fast.**

57

I wanted to go.	/wantid/
She wanted to go.	/wanid/
We needed to buy one.	/ni:did/
He asked her.	/aster/
She asked him.	/astim/

3 **Check the boxes of the activities you sometimes do on the weekend. Add two other activities of your own.**

- ☐ watch TV
- ☐ do the laundry
- ☐ take a drive
- ☐ see a movie
- ☐ hang out with a friend
- ☐ do homework
- ☐ take it easy
- ☐ ______________
- ☐ cook a meal
- ☐ go for a walk
- ☐ go shopping
- ☐ work at your part-time job
- ☐ go to karaoke
- ☐ play a musical instrument
- ☐ clean your room
- ☐ ______________

4 **First practice the conversation below. Then ask about the activities in Activity 3 that you did last weekend. When you answer 'yes' give more details.**

58

A: Did you watch TV last weekend?

B: No, I didn't.

A: Did you go shopping?

B: Yes, I did. I bought a coat. It wasn't expensive.

A: Did you cook a meal?

B: Yes, I did. I cooked *yakimeshi*, fried rice.

5 **Draw lines to match the statements on the left with the correct replies on the right. Then practice with a partner.**

If your friend says ...	You reply ...
My bicycle was stolen.	That sounds like fun.
I slept all day on Sunday.	Oh, that's too bad!
Not much happened this weekend.	Wow! That's terrible!
The weather was beautiful.	I see.
On Sunday I met friends for lunch.	That's nice.
I caught a cold.	Really? You're kidding!

6 Pronunciation: Listen to these expressions and then practice saying them. Notice that 'did you' can change to /didja/ and even just /ja/ at speed. Here we practice the two fast forms.

59

Where did you go?	☞	Where didja go?	☞	Where ja go?
Who did you meet?	☞	Who didja meet?	☞	Who ja meet?
Where did you eat?	☞	Where didja eat?	☞	Where ja eat?

7 Read about Akemi's weekend. Then write about your weekend. (Make it up if you want to.) Next talk about your weekend with a partner.

I had lunch with a friend in Shinsaibashi. We went to an Italian restaurant. It was very good. Then we went window shopping. I couldn't find anything I wanted to buy. In the evening I worked from six o'clock to ten. I was very tired.

8 Listening: **Kevin and Sue talk about the weekend. Listen to their conversation and write the answers to the questions in the blanks.**

60

a. What did Kevin do on Saturday afternoon? ______________________

b. What did Kevin do in the evening? ______________________

c. What did Sue do on Saturday? ______________________

d. What did Sue do on Sunday? ______________________

9 Speaking: **First, write your answers to the questions below. Then ask the questions in pairs and take notes on your partner's answers. Change partners and do it again.**

Questions	You	Partner 1 (Name:_____)	Partner 2 (Name:_____)	Partner 3 (Name:_____)
a. How was your weekend?				
b. What did you do?				
c. What time did you get home?				
d. How was your day yesterday?				
e. Did you buy anything?				
f. What did you have for dinner?				
g. Did you do any homework?				
h. What time did you get up today?				
i. What did you have for breakfast?				

Unit 10

Have you ever been abroad?

1 Check the boxes of the activities you can do. Add an activity of your own.

Can you …

- ☐ … drive a car?
- ☐ … cook a simple dish?
- ☐ … play a musical instrument?
- ☐ … ski or snowboard?
- ☐ … speak a foreign language?
- ☐ … use a computer well?
- ☐ … sing well?
- ☐ … save money?
- ☐ … ______________________________

Useful Language

I'm good at … (ing).

I'm bad at … (ing).

2 Listening: As you listen to the conversation below, fill in the blanks. Then practice it with a partner.

61

A: Can you ________________________?

B: No, I can't. ____.

How about you?

A: Yes, I can, but not very well.

____.

B: That's great. Uh, can you ________________________________?

A: I can play the piano a little. ____.

B: I can't play anything. ____________________________.

A: It's never too late to learn.

Common Mistake

× I'm a paper driver.

✓ I have a driver's license but I don't drive.

3 **Speaking:** **Using Activity 2 as a model, ask and answer about things you can do using these topics. Take notes on your partner's answers.**

… drive a car? ________________

… play a musical instrument? ________________

… speak a foreign language? ________________

… sing well? ________________

… cook a simple dish? ________________

… ski or snowboard? ________________

… use a computer well? ________________

… save money? ________________

________________ ________________

4 **Grammar:** **Write the past form and past participle form of these verbs in the spaces. Add two more verbs.**

Verb base form	Past form	Past participle form
play	played	played
see	saw	seen
go		
make		
wear		
hear		
meet		
teach		
take		
buy		
ride		
write		
quit		

5 Pronunciation: **When saying these words the mouth goes to the position to say t or d but just pronounces /n/. Listen and practice.**

62

eaten	written	listen	button
cotton	ridden	sudden	Aladdin

6 **Check the boxes of things that you have done. Make one new question.**

- ☐ Have you ever been to Disneyland?
- ☐ Have you ever been to USJ?
- ☐ Have you had a cold recently?
- ☐ Have you ever eaten Indian food?
- ☐ Have you worn *yukata* recently?
- ☐ Have you ever been abroad?
- ☐ Have you missed a class recently?
- ☐ Have you seen a movie recently?
- ☐ Have you ever been to a baseball game?
- ☐ Have you ever been to Hokkaido or Okinawa?
- ☐ Have you been to the dentist recently?
- ☐ ______________________________

7 Speaking: **Practice the conversation.**

63

A: Have you ever been to Disneyland?

B: Yes, I have. I went in March, with a friend from high school. We had a lot of fun. How about you?

A: Um, no, I haven't. Not my kind of thing.

B: Oh, I see. Uh, have you had a cold recently?

A: I have one now. I get a lot of colds.

B: That's too bad. I hope you feel better soon.

8 Listening: **Shiho and Masaki discuss a few topics. Write answers to the questions in the blanks.**

64

a. Has Shiho ever been to a baseball game?

____

b. When did Masaki go to Hawaii?

____

c. Has Shiho been to the dentist recently?

____

d. Has Masaki missed a class recently?

____

9 Speaking: **Make a group of three. Use Activity 7 as a model and ask and answer the questions in Activity 6. Take notes on your partners' answers. Then join with another student and tell about the two people you talked to.**

Partner 1

Partner 2

Unit 11

What kinds of movies do you like?

1 Pronunciation: **The letter 'a' can sound different depending on the word it's in. Listen and practice.**

65

/wɔːr/	war	warm	warning	award
/eɪ/	ancient	label	matrix	stadium

2 Vocabulary: **Circle the words you don't know. Check their meanings in a dictionary.**

disappointing	dull	funny	imaginative
moving	powerful	scary	violent
interesting	strange	confusing	exciting

Common Error

Remember: "Fun" does not mean funny.
"Fun" means enjoyable.
"Funny" means something that makes you laugh.

Examples: That party was a lot of fun.
That comedian is really funny.

3 **Do you understand these common questions about movies? Research a movie and fill in the information. Ask and answer in pairs to fill in your partner's information.**

Questions	Your movie	Your partner's movie
a. Who's in this movie?		
b. What's this movie about?		
c. Where's this movie playing?		
d. Have you read any reviews?		
e. Is this movie based on a book?		

4 Listening: **As you listen to the conversation below, fill in the blanks. Then practice it with a partner.**

66

A: I saw ______________________________ last week.

B: You mean, the live-action movie with ________________?

A: Yes. And Naomi Scott.

B: ____?

A: Uh, I liked it a lot. It's fun.

B: Maybe I should see it.
I saw *A Star is Born* on Netflix a month ago.

A: I haven't seen it. ____________________?

B: Good. It was very ______________.

A: ____________________?

B: Bradley Cooper and Lady Gaga.

A: I like both of them.

5 **Which of these movies have you seen? Circle the ones you've seen. Use the model in Activity 4 to tell your partner about movies you've seen.**

Finding Nemo	Avatar	Spirited Away
Frozen	The Matrix	Pirates of the Caribbean
Star Wars	Tangled (Rapunzel)	Beauty and the Beast
The Greatest Showman	Captain Marvel	Toy Story 4
Avengers: Endgame	Aladdin	Demon Slayer
____________________	____________________	

6 Listening: **Listen to Hina and Jun talk about movies. Listen to their conversation and write the answers to these questions in the blanks.**

67

a. What kinds of movies does Jun like?

____

b. What kinds of movies does Hina dislike?

____

c. Where does Jun like to see movies?

____

d. What is Hina's complaint?

____

7 Speaking: **Ask these questions to find out about your partner and movies. Write notes using your partner's answers in the blanks.**

a. Do you watch a lot of movies? ______________________________

b. How do you watch them? In a theater or at home? ______________________________

c. Have you seen a movie recently? ______________________________

d. Is there a movie you want to see? ______________________________

e. Do you prefer watching movies at the theater or at home? ______________________________

f. Can you recommend a movie? ______________________________

g. What Disney movie do you like best? ______________________________

h. What Ghibli movie do you like best? ______________________________

i. Which do you like better, movies with subtitles or ones dubbed into Japanese?

____

8 **Seeing a movie is a popular activity when meeting friends or going on a date. Look at this list of activities. Check the boxes of those you have done or would like to do.**

☐ see a movie
☐ go out for dinner
☐ take a walk in a park
☐ go to a concert
☐ go to karaoke
☐ go to a theme park
☐ visit a temple or shrine
☐ get together for coffee/tea
☐ go shopping for clothes
☐ play pachinko
☐ go see a baseball game
☐ ______________________________

9 Listening: As you listen to this conversation fill in the blanks. Then practice it with a partner. Next, practice it again several times using the activities you checked in Activity 8.

68

A: What do you like to do when meeting up with friends?

B: I like to ____________________ for coffee or tea.
It gives you lots of time to talk.

A: I don't know. That can be boring. I like doing something more active.
I like to ________________________________.

B: I see. What else do you like to do?

A: Well, I like to ________________________________.

B: Really? I like to ____.

10 Speaking: Write your answers to these questions. Then ask three partners the questions and take notes on their answers. Then report to a new partner.

Questions	You	Partner 1 (Name:______)	Partner 2 (Name:______)	Partner 3 (Name:______)
a. Who's your favorite comedian?	________	________	________	________
b. Who's a comedian you don't think is funny?	________	________	________	________
c. What's your favorite TV show?	________	________	________	________
d. Do you read much?	________	________	________	________
e. Do you spend much time using a computer?	________	________	________	________
f. Who's your favorite solo artist or music group?	________	________	________	________
g. Where do you like to shop for clothes?	________	________	________	________

Unit 12

What's the weather going to be like?

1 Vocabulary: **Which words can you use to describe the pictures? Write them on the lines.**

Weather words

a. It's sunny.
b. It's cloudy.
c. It's windy.
d. It's foggy.
e. It's rainy (raining).
f. It's snowing.
g. It's hot.
h. It's cold.
i. It's a bit cool/warm.
j. It's nice and cool/warm.
k. It's humid.

______ ______ ______

______ ______ ______

2 Pronunciation: **"Going to" changes to "gonna" at speed. Listen and then practice these expressions.**

69

It's going to be hot.	It's gonna be hot.
It's going to rain.	It's gonna rain.
They say it's going to be cold.	They say it's gonna be cold.
They say it's going to snow.	They say it's gonna snow.

3 Speaking: **Practice this conversation with a partner.**

70

A: What's the weather going to be like today?
B: This morning it was very cold but it's going to be nice and sunny later.
A: How about tomorrow?
B: They say it's going to be cold and rainy.
A: Oh. That's not good.

4 Speaking: **Join with a partner to make conversations using these questions. Add a question of your own. Take notes on your partner's answers.**

a. What's the weather going to be like later today? ____________________

b. How about this evening? ____________________

c. What's it going to be like tomorrow? ____________________

d. What's your favorite kind of weather? ____________________

e. What do you think of the Japanese summer? ____________________

f. Do you mind the cold in winter? ____________________

g. Does weather affect your mood? ____________________

h. ____________________? ____________________

5 Pronunciation: **Important words get stress in English. Listen to the recording and then practice it.**

71 I checked the weather in Osaka for today. The high is going to be nine degrees. The low is going to be four degrees. There's a sixty percent chance of rain in the afternoon.

6 Speaking: **Use your phones. Student A should research New York, Naha and another city. Student B should research Bangkok, Sapporo and another city. Tell your partner what you found using the model of Activity 5.**

Student A

	Tokyo	New York	Naha	______
High Temperature	25°C	______	______	______
Low Temperature	18°C	______	______	______
Chance of Rain	50%	______	______	______

Student B

	Tokyo	Bangkok	Sapporo	______
High Temperature	25°C	______	______	______
Low Temperature	18°C	______	______	______
Chance of Rain	50%	______	______	______

7

Speaking: **Check the boxes of the health problems you sometimes have. Practice the conversation. Then practice it again with the different health problems.**

72

- ☐ a cold
- ☐ a cough
- ☐ a stomachache
- ☐ a runny nose
- ☐ hay fever
- ☐ a sore throat
- ☐ a headache
- ☐ the flu
- ☐ a toothache

A: Are you OK? You don't look very well.

B: Actually, I have a bad cold.

A: That's too bad. I hope you get over it soon.

B: Thanks.

8

Here is a list of things you might do when sick. Check the boxes of those things you have done before. Write one thing not on the list in the blank. Practice the conversation. Then practice again with the health problems in Activity 7.

73

- ☐ go to the doctor
- ☐ stay in bed
- ☐ take medicine
- ☐ take a nap
- ☐ take a day off
- ☐ take a hot bath
- ☐ wear a mask
- ☐ put up with it
- ☐ other: ____________________

A: What do you do when you have a cold?

B: I don't go to the doctor. It usually takes a lot of time. I just put up with it.

A: Me too.

B: What do you do when you have a headache?

A: I take medicine. I try to take a nap.

B: I never get a headache.

We usually say "take medicine" (not "drink medicine.")

9

Listening: **Hannah and Daniel talk about health. Listen to their conversation and write the answers to these questions in the blanks.**

74

a. What does Hannah have for breakfast? ____________________

b. Why does Daniel skip breakfast? ____________________

c. Why does Hannah not go to the doctor? ____________________

d. Is going to the doctor cheaper in the US or in Japan? ____________________

10 Speaking: **Do you have a healthy lifestyle? Answer the following questions (add one of your own) by putting a check mark in the boxes where the answer is YES. Then interview two other partners and mark their YES answers too.**

Do you ...	You	Partner 1 (Name:________)	Partner 2 (Name:________)
... eat breakfast every morning?	☐	☐	☐
... usually get 7 to 8 hours of sleep?	☐	☐	☐
... avoid eating junk food?	☐	☐	☐
... eat enough vegetables?	☐	☐	☐
... get exercise?	☐	☐	☐
... often go to the doctor?	☐	☐	☐
... usually feel happy with your life?	☐	☐	☐
... other: ____________________	☐	☐	☐
YES Answers (total)	________	________	________

Who has the healthiest lifestyle in your group?

____

What habits should you change to be more healthy?

Example: I should eat more vegetables.

____

____

____

____

Unit 13

What's your favorite coffee shop?

1 Vocabulary: **Check the boxes of the places you can find in your neighborhood.**

- ☐ a beauty parlor
- ☐ a drugstore
- ☐ a temple
- ☐ a shrine
- ☐ a supermarket
- ☐ a convenience store
- ☐ a department store
- ☐ a liquor store
- ☐ a bank
- ☐ a bakery
- ☐ a stationery store
- ☐ a restaurant
- ☐ a kindergarten
- ☐ an elementary school
- ☐ ______________________

Complete these sentences. Then tell your partner about your neighborhood.

In my neighborhood there's a/an ______________________

In my neighborhood there are a few ______________________

In my neighborhood there are no ______________________

2 Listening: **Kaoru and Shoji talk about where they live. Listen and write answers to the questions.**

75

a. Who does Kaoru live with? ______________________

b. Who does Shoji live with? ______________________

c. How does Shoji get to the station? ______________________

d. What places are in Shoji's neighborhood? ______________________

3 Speaking: **Talk with a partner about his/her neighborhood. Write down your partner's answers.**

a. Where do you live? ______________________________

b. Do you live in a house or an apartment? ______________________________

c. What's your neighborhood like? ______________________________

What buildings are there? ______________________________

Is it noisy or quiet? ______________________________

d. Do you talk to your neighbors? ______________________________

e. How far is the nearest station? ______________________________

f. Is there a good restaurant? ______________________________

Useful Language

We say hello.

We don't say hello.

4 Speaking: **Practice the conversation with a partner.**

76

A: Excuse me. I'm looking for the library.

B: The library? Do you see that building over there?
The big white one on the left. That's the library.

A: I got it. Thanks a lot.

B: You're welcome.

Useful Language

on the left / on the right

It's on the second floor.

It's that way.

5 **Pretend you're at the gate to your school. Stand up and in turns ask and answer about places on campus using the model of Activity 4. Use body language!**

the library	the cafeteria	the *kyomuka* (Educational Affairs Section)
the IT center	the gym	________________

6 Listening: **Listen and write in the prices you hear.**

1. ¥ ________ 2. ¥ ________ 3. ¥ ________ 4. ¥ ________

7 **Decide which person is Student A and B. Cover your partner's section. Say the prices to your partner. Write the prices your partner says in the blanks.**

Student A

1. ¥250	2. ¥1,900	3. ¥3,400	4. ¥20,000
5. ¥1,500	6. ¥2,250	7. ¥10	8. ¥15,827
1. ¥ ________	2. ¥ ________	3. ¥ ________	4. ¥ ________
5. ¥ ________	6. ¥ ________	7. ¥ ________	8. ¥ ________

Student B

1. ¥ ________	2. ¥ ________	3. ¥ ________	4. ¥ ________
5. ¥ ________	6. ¥ ________	7. ¥ ________	8. ¥ ________
1. ¥480	2. ¥950	3. ¥1,200	4. ¥32,000
5. ¥4,300	6. ¥8,000	7. ¥25	8. ¥10,232

8 Pronunciation: **Sometimes we stress a word which isn't so important for meaning.**

Where is it?

Who is it?

How much is it?

How much were they?

9 **Listening:** **Sasha and John talk about Sasha's favorite coffee shop. Write her answers to the questions in the spaces.**

79

a. What's the name of the coffee shop? ____________________

b. What's the atmosphere like? ____________________

c. What does Sasha order? ____________________

d. How much is it? ____________________

10 **Speaking:** **Write your own answers to the following questions. Then talk with three partners and take notes on their answers.**

Questions	You	Partner 1 (Name:______)	Partner 2 (Name:______)	Partner 3 (Name:______)
a. What's your favorite coffee shop?	______	______	______	______
b. Where is it?	______	______	______	______
c. What's it like?	______	______	______	______
d. How often do you go there?	______	______	______	______
e. Is it expensive?	______	______	______	______
f. What do you usually order?	______	______	______	______
g. How much is it?	______	______	______	______

Unit 14 Do you have a part-time job?

1 Vocabulary: **How did you feel about your high school subjects? Practice saying these words and then put them into the three categories below.**

Japanese	English	mathematics
classical Japanese	science	biology
physics	chemistry	physical education (P.E.)
history	geography	social studies
music	calligraphy	

I liked it	It was okay	I didn't like it
____________	____________	____________
____________	____________	____________
____________	____________	____________
____________	____________	____________

2 Listening: **As you listen to the conversation below, fill in the blanks. Then practice it with a partner.**

80

A: Where did you go to high school?

B: Uh, I went to high school in Kagoshima. ____________________ in the city.

A: ________! I went to our school's high school. So what subject did you like best?

B: I liked Japanese history. ____________________ for me.

A: Japanese history? I liked ____________. We had a great teacher.

B: Did you play sports?

A: I played ____________ in junior high school but not in high school.

3 Listening: **Listen to Sakura and Hiko talk about their high schools. Write answers to the questions.**

81

a. What subject did Sakura like best?

b. What subject did Hiko like best?

c. Did Hiko wear a uniform?

d. Was Sakura's school co-ed (co-educational)?

4 Speaking: **Discuss your own high school. Ask and answer the questions in pairs. Take notes on your partner's answers.**

a. Where did you go to high school?

b. Did you enjoy it?

c. Was it a strict school or was it relaxed?

d. Did you wear a uniform?

e. Was it co-ed?

f. What subject did you like best?

g. Was there any subject you didn't like?

h. Did you play sports?

Useful Language

a navy blue blazer

an all-boys/all-girls school

5 Pronunciation: **/iː/ These words are often mispronounced by Japanese students. First listen and then practice saying them.**

82

media meter theme comedian premium

6 Vocabulary: **What are popular part-time jobs for university students? Brainstorm a few.**

______________ ______________ ______________

______________ ______________ ______________

______________ ______________ ______________

7 Listening: **Reina and Naoya talk about their part-time jobs. Take notes on their answers.**

83

a. How often does Reina work?

____

b. What subjects does Naoya teach?

____

c. When did Naoya start working?

____

d. What's Naoya's pay?

____

e. Why does Reina like her job?

____

8 Speaking: **Write your answers to these questions. Then ask three partners the questions and take notes on their answers.**

Questions	You	Partner 1 (Name:______)	Partner 2 (Name:______)	Partner 3 (Name:______)
a. Do you have a part-time job?				
b. Why did you choose that job?				
c. How far is it from your home?				
d. Do you like it?				
e. How long have you been doing it?				
f. What's the pay?				
g. How much do you make a month?				
h. What do you do with the money you make?				
i. Are you friendly with your co-workers?				
j. Do you ever go out with them?				
k. Have you ever made a mistake at your job?				
l. ______________________				

Useful Language

I've gotten used to it.

I can eat for free.

Unit 15 How long have you had your phone?

1 Pronunciation: **The letter 'o' can sound different depending on the word it's in.**

84

/oʊ/	home	most	only	open
/ɑː/	not	coffee	hot	problem
/ʌ/	love	month	glove	above

2 Vocabulary: **Match the appliances with their pictures. Write the letters on the lines under the pictures. Circle the things you have in your house. Add one more thing.**

a. electronic dictionary	b. computer	c. tablet
d. television (TV)	e. microwave	f. robot vacuum
g. smart speaker	h. headphones	________________

____

____

____

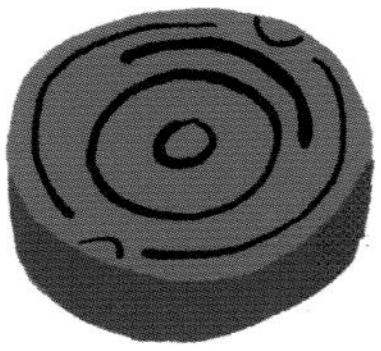
____

____

____

____

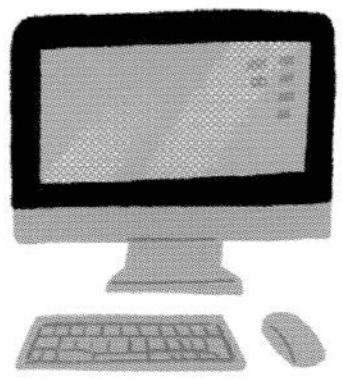
____

I have one and am happy with it:

________________________ ________________________

I want one or need a new one:

________________________ ________________________

I don't have one but don't need or want one:

________________________ ________________________

3 **Practice the conversation. Then ask and answer about the products in Activity 2.**

85

A: Do you have a computer?

B: Yeah, I do. It's new. I just bought it three months ago.
How about you?

A: We have a computer at home. I don't use it much.
My phone is enough for me. Uh, do you have a tablet?

B: No, I don't. I don't need one.

4 **In pairs, decide who is Student A and Student B. Cover your partner's numbers. Say your numbers and your partner should write them in the blanks.**

Student A

1. 15,000	2. 8,500	3. 70,000
4. 45,000	5. 18,000	6. 200,000

1. ____________	2. ____________	3. ____________
4. ____________	5. ____________	6. ____________

Student B

1. ____________	2. ____________	3. ____________
4. ____________	5. ____________	6. ____________

1. 50,000	2. 9,200	3. 125,000
4. 16,000	5. 48,000	6. 7,500

5 **Practice the conversation. Then make up a new one using different information.**

86

A: How long have you had your phone?

B: I've had it for ... let's see ... nearly two years.
The contract runs out in two months.

A: Two months? How much is the monthly bill?

B: I think it's about 8,000 yen.

A: 8,000. So ... are there any problems with it?

B: I dropped it yesterday and broke the screen.

A: Oh, no! That's too bad.

6 Internet acronyms: What do the following acronyms mean?

ez ____________

b4 ____________

cu ______ ____________

idk I ______ ____________

btw by ______ ____________

omw on ______ ____________

dw don't ____________

omg ______ ____________ ____________

lol ____________ ______ ____________

imo ______ ______ ____________

Some others:

ttyl talk to ______ ____________

yolo you only ____________ ____________

sup ____________ ______?

7 Practice the conversation.

87

A: I just got a text from Frank.

B: What does it say?

A: RUOK? CUL8R.

B: IC.

8 Listening: Listen to Neal and Kim talk about their phones. Write answers to the questions.

88

a. How long has Neal had his phone?

____

b. How long has Kim had her phone?

____

c. Is Kim careful with her phone?

____

d. What does Neal do with his phone on the train?

____

e. What does Kim use her phone for?

____

9 **Speaking:** **In pairs discuss your phone. Take notes on your partner's answers and then change partners.**

Questions	Partner 1 (Name:______)	Partner 2 (Name:______)	Partner 3 (Name:______)
a. Do you have an iPhone or an Android phone?			
b. How long have you had it?			
c. What do you like about LINE?			
d. What other apps do you use?			
e. Do you use Twitter? Do you ever tweet?			
f. Do you use Instagram?			
g. What games do you play?			
h. Are there any problems with your phone?			

Unit 16

What kind of clothes do you like to wear?

1 Vocabulary: **English words borrowed into Japanese often drop the more important second part of a word or phrase. For example "department store" becomes *depaato*.**

a department store	the front desk
a (one-piece) dress	a (knitted) sweater
(pierced) earrings	a (bargain) sale

2 Vocabulary: **What useful vocabulary for clothes and accessories can you think of?**

a shirt	pants
socks	sneakers
a ring	

3 Speaking: **Look around the class. What are people wearing? What colors are they wearing? Ask and answer using these questions.**

a. What's <u>Hikaru</u> wearing? ______________________

b. Who's wearing black? ______________________

Who's wearing navy? ______________________

c. Is anyone wearing gray? ______________________

d. What color is your bag? ______________________

e. What colors do you often wear? ______________________

f. What colors do you avoid? ______________________

4 Pronunciation: Practice these expressions of surprise and annoyance. Put some feeling into it!

89

5 Listening: Listen to the conversation and fill in the blanks. Then practice the conversation.

90

A: Ooh! I like your ____________ !
Is it new?

B: No, I've had it ____________________.
Those are nice jeans. Where did you ____________________ ?

A: I got them at Uniqlo.

B: ______________________________ ?

A: Let me think. I think they were about ____________________ yen.

B: Gee! That's a good price.

6 Speaking: Compliment your partner using the model of Activity 5.

I like your shirt.
Oh! Cool shirt!
That's a nice top/dress.
Those are nice shoes/glasses/jeans.
Where did you get it/them?
Was it/Were they expensive?
How much was it/were they?

7 Pronunciation: **Some consonants are silent. First listen and then practice saying these words.**

91

height /háɪt/	weight /wéɪt/
months /mʌ́ns/	receipt /rɪsíːt/
comfortable /kʌ́mftəbl/	clothes /klóʊz/

8 Listening: **Listen to Chris and Wendy talk about clothes. Write answers to the questions.**

92

a. What colors does Chris like?

____

b. What's Wendy's favorite color?

____

c. What color does Chris avoid?

____

d. What's Wendy's shoe size?

____

e. When did Chris buy his jacket?

____

9 Speaking: **Talk with a partner about clothes. Take notes on the answers your partner gives. Then report to a new partner.**

a. What kind of clothes do you like to wear?

____

b. What colors do you like?

____

c. Where do you go shopping for clothes?

____

d. Do you ever buy clothes online?

____

e. Do you ever have to wear a uniform?

____

f. Do you find it easy to get shoes you like?

____

g. What are your favorite clothes to wear?

____

Conversation Game Rules

1. Join a group of 3 or 4 students. One person starts by flipping a coin.
2. If it's a number, move 1 space.
3. If it's a figure, move 2 spaces.

START

1
How do you spell your first name?

2
What's your major?

3
What time do you usually get up?

4
What time do you usually go to bed?

5
Where are you from?

6
What's your favorite food?

7
What do you drink at breakfast?

8
What's your favorite kind of music?

9
Can you play a musical instrument?

10
How often do you get your hair cut?

11
Which is the hottest month in Japan?

12
Do you prefer tea or coffee?

13
What time did you get up today?

4. Look clockwise: The person on your left will ask you the question.

5. Answer the question. If you can answer, you can stay on the space. If you cannot answer, use your textbook to review and go back to your original position.

Useful expressions:
I'll go first.　私から始めますね。　Is it my turn?　私の番ですか？　It's your turn.　あなたの番です。

22
What are you wearing today?

23
How did you like this game?

21
What games do you play on your phone?

20
Do you have a part-time job?

19
What's your favorite coffee shop?

18
Do you often feel tired?

17
What's the weather like today?

14
Can you drive a car?

15
Have you ever been to DisneySea?

16
What kinds of movies do you like?

For further English practice use the website found at:

https://www.ericbray.com/eric-brays-english-study-resource-online/

ERIC BRAY'S

English Study Resources

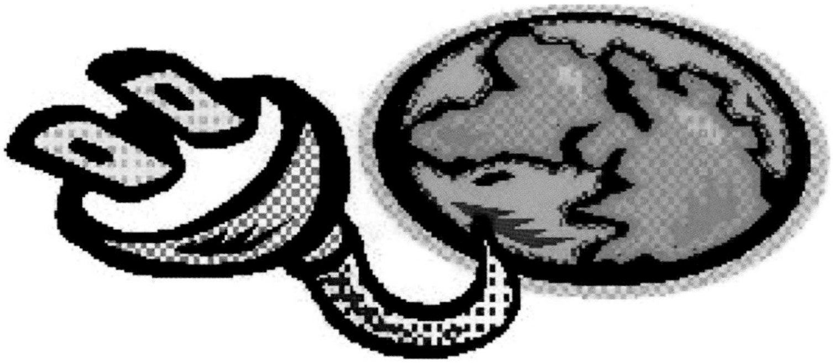

Listening

Pronunciation

Reading

Chat Opportunities

Grammar

Culture

Dictionaries

Quizzes and Games

New Getting Into English

New Getting Into English [B-918]
始めよう英会話！ ＜改訂新版＞

1 刷 2021 年 1 月 30 日
2 刷 2023 年 3 月 31 日

著　者 Joseph Cronin ジョセフ・クローニン
Eric Bray エリック・ブレイ

発行者 南雲　一範 Kazunori Nagumo
発行所 株式会社　南雲堂
〒162-0801 東京都新宿区山吹町361
NAN'UN-DO Co., Ltd.
361 Yamabuki-cho, Shinjuku-ku, Tokyo 162-0801, Japan
振替口座：00160-0-46863
TEL: 03-3268-2311（営業部：学校関係）
03-3268-2384（営業部：書店関係）
03-3268-2387（編集部）
FAX: 03-3269-2486
編集者 加藤　敦

組　版 中西　史子

イラスト ヨシオカ ユリ

装　丁 銀　月　堂

検　印 省　　略

コード ISBN978-4-523-17918-4 C0082

Printed in Japan

E-mail : nanundo@post.email.ne.jp
URL : https://www.nanun-do.co.jp/